O
Colors!

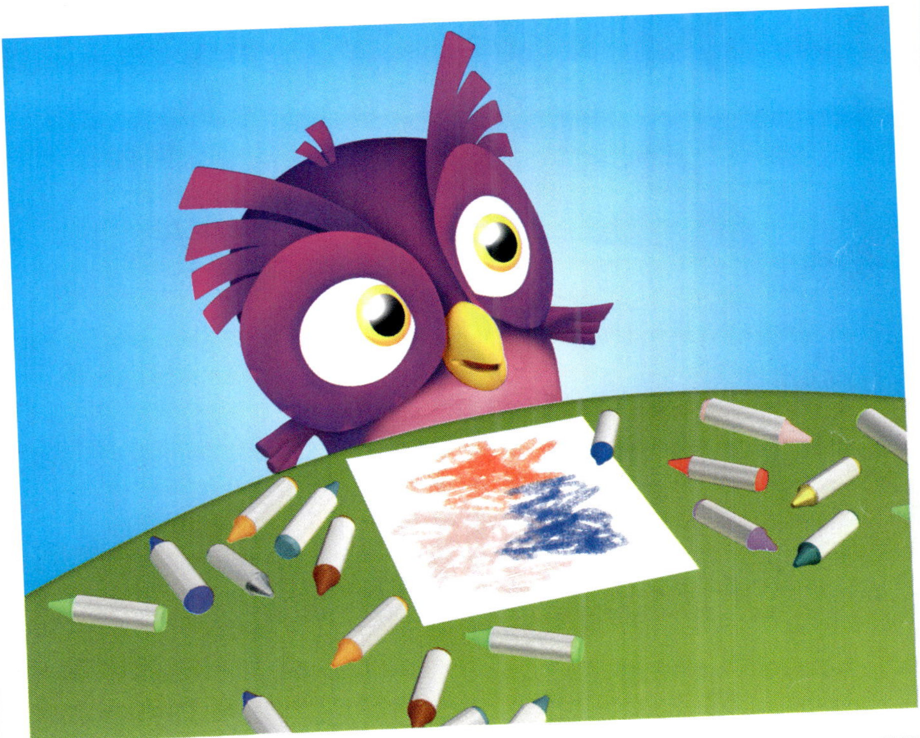

PEARSON

Glenview, Illinois • Boston, Massachusetts
Chandler, Arizona • Upper Saddle River, New Jersey

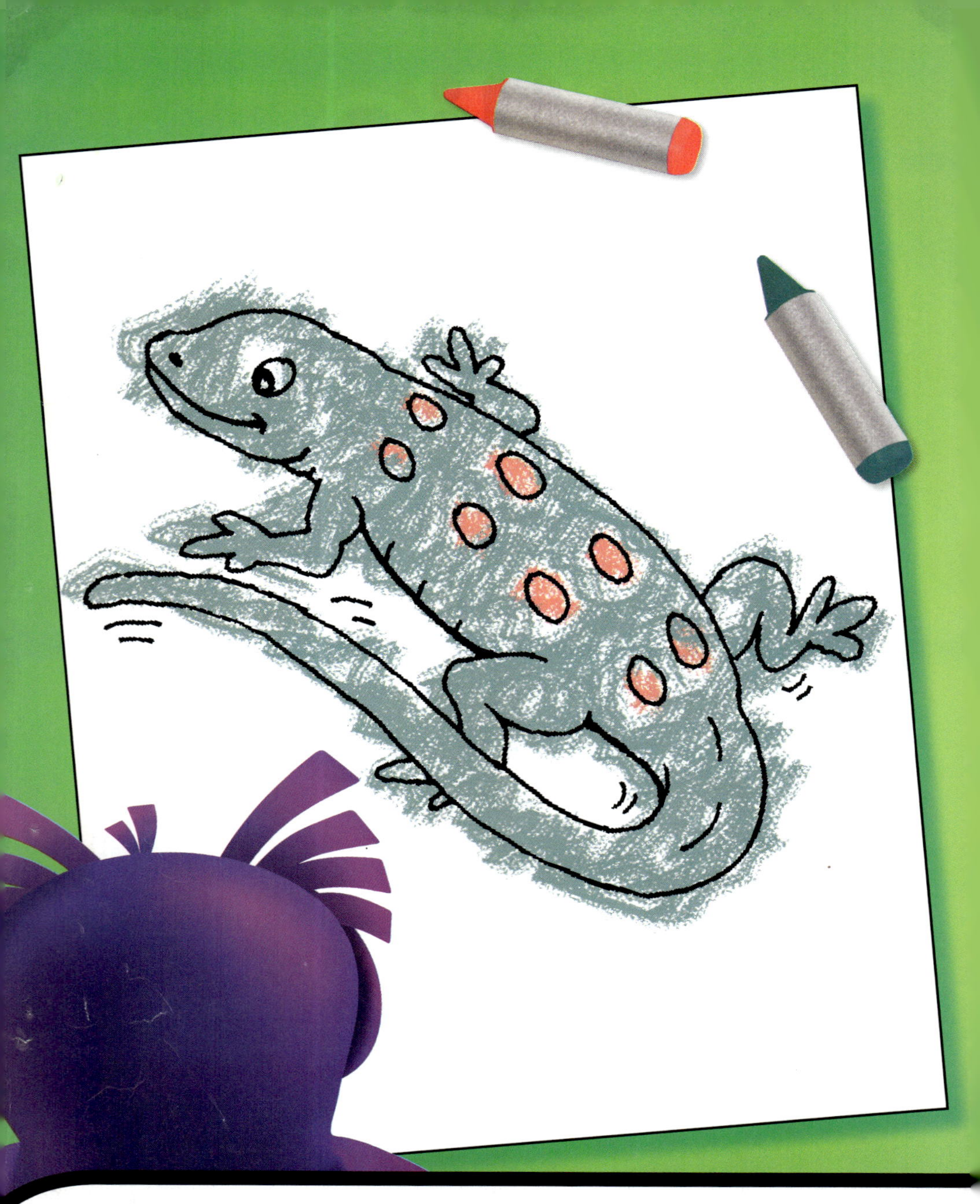

lizard

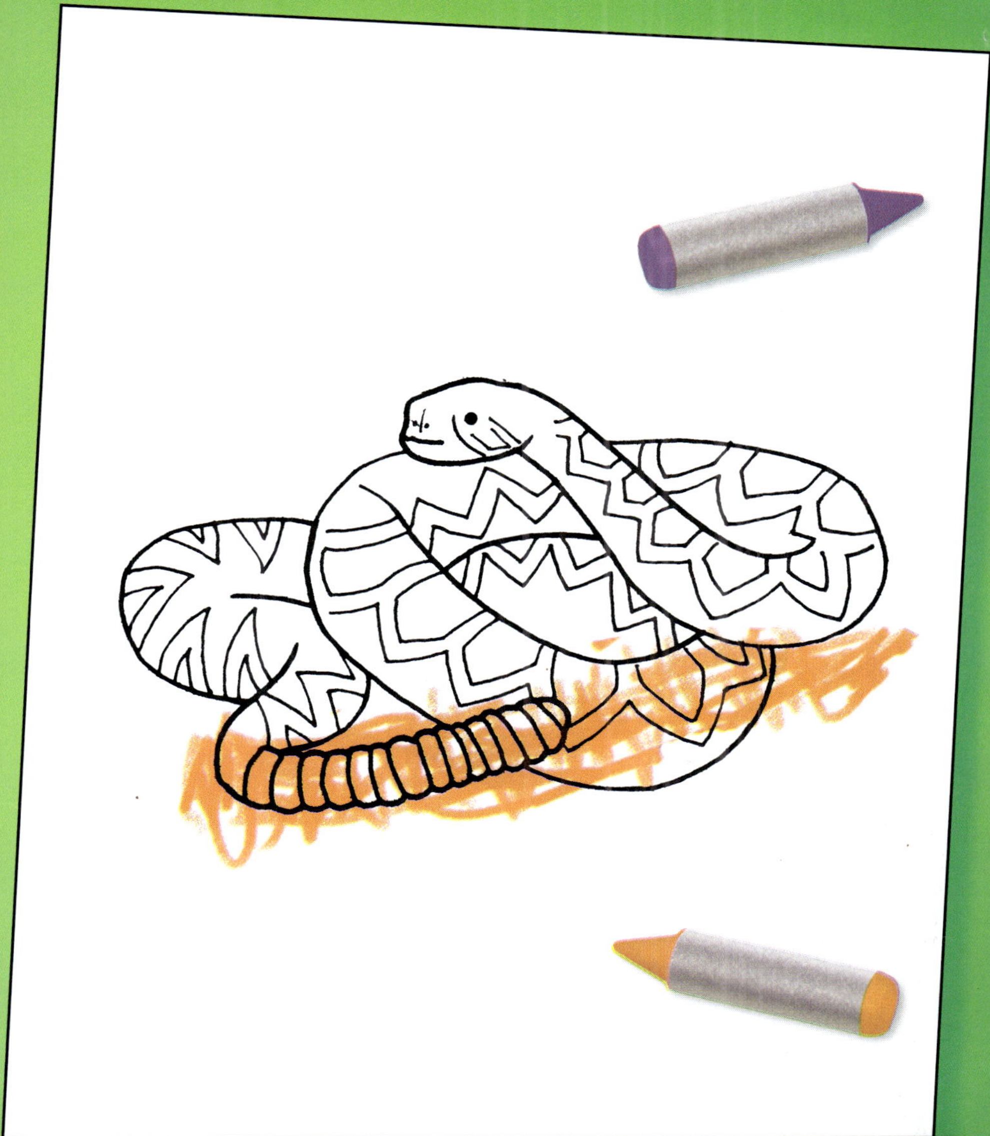

snake

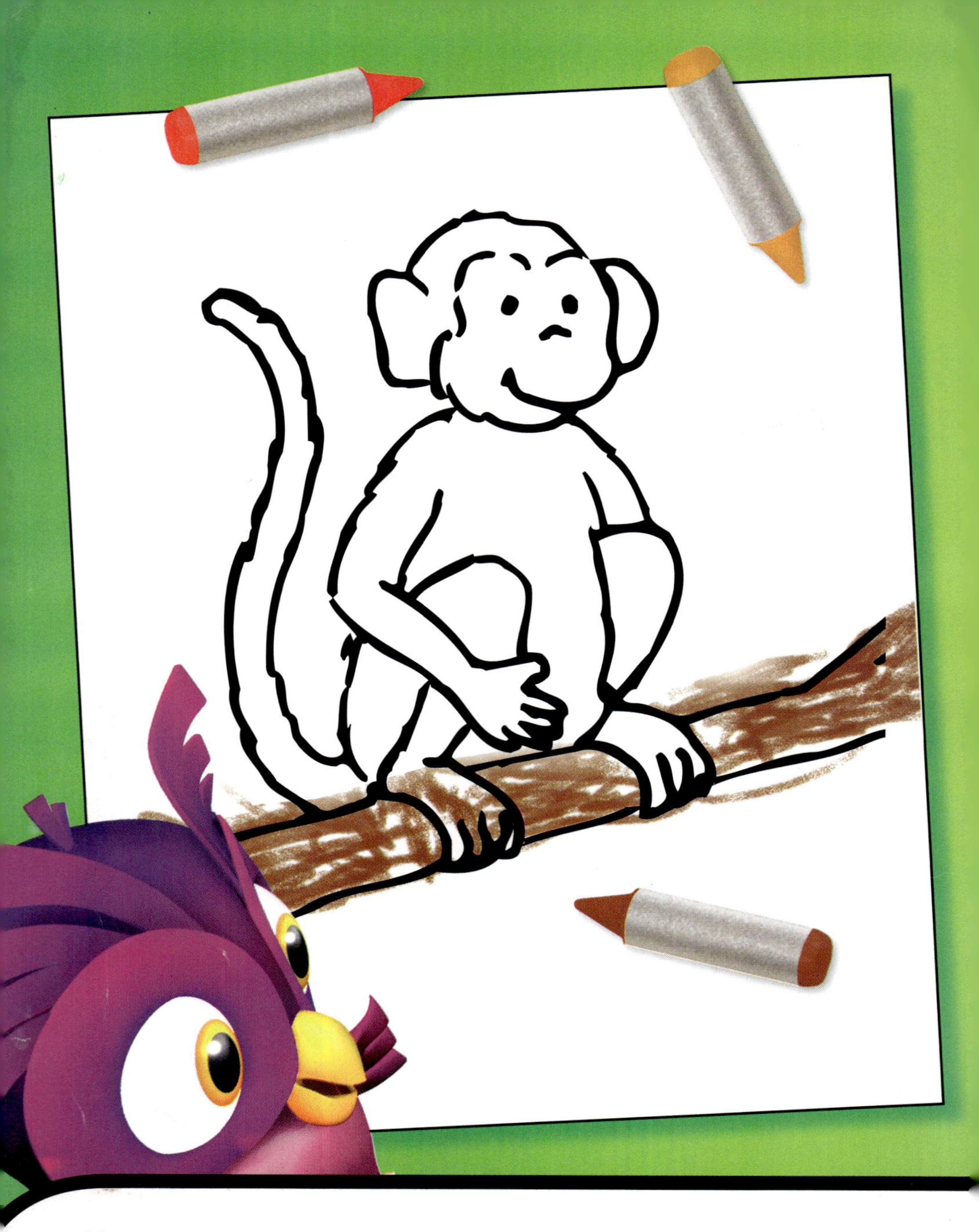

monkey

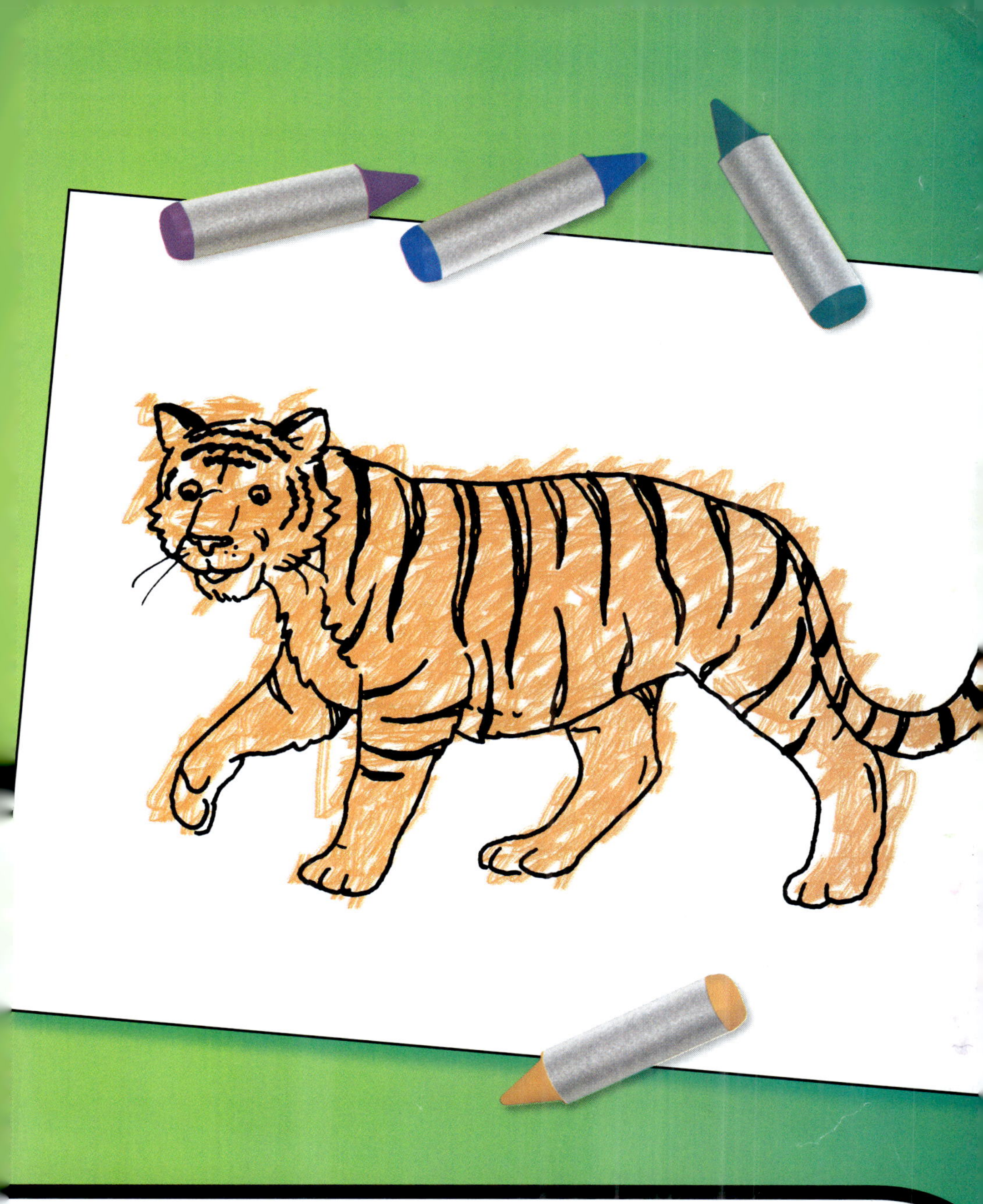

tiger

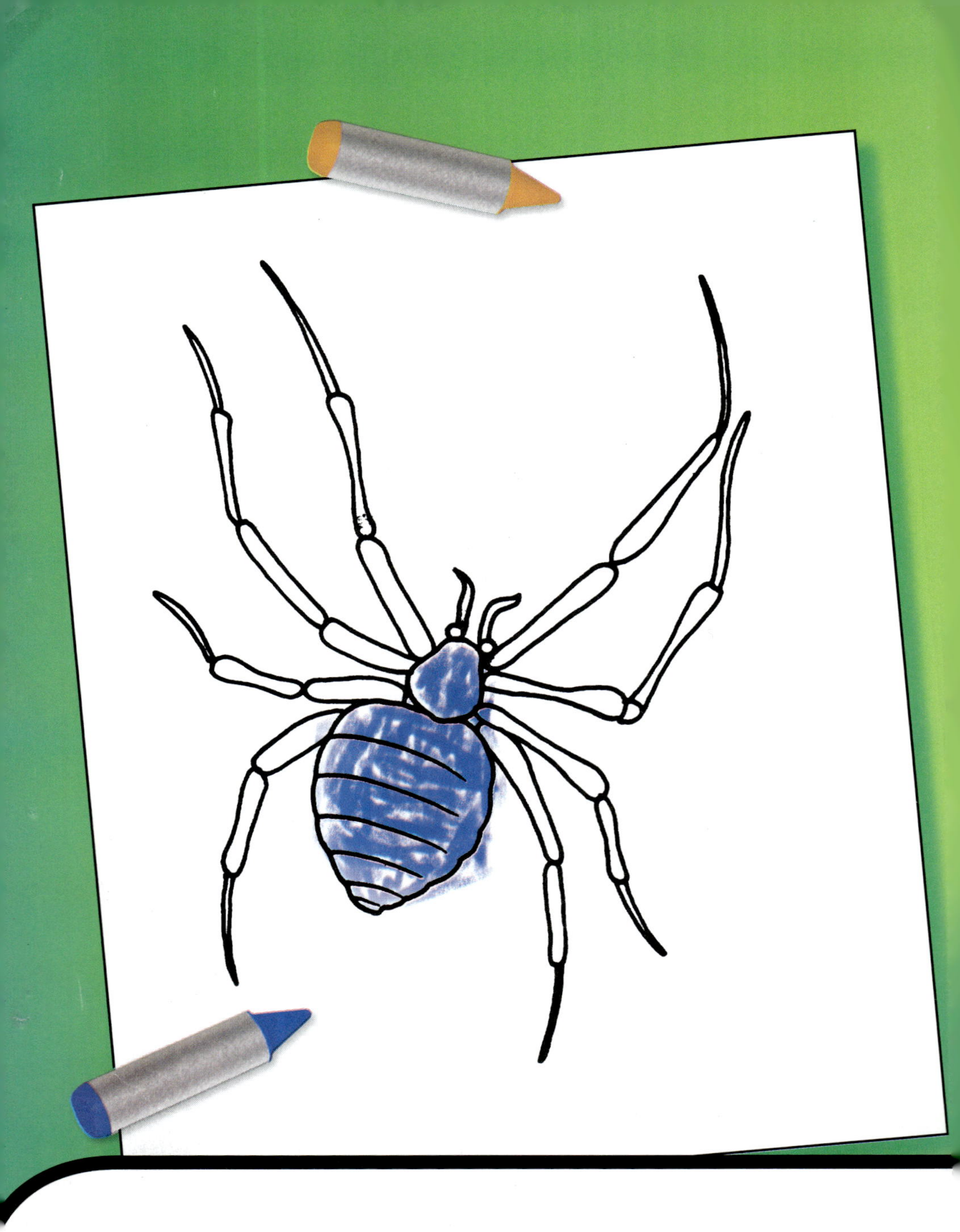

spider

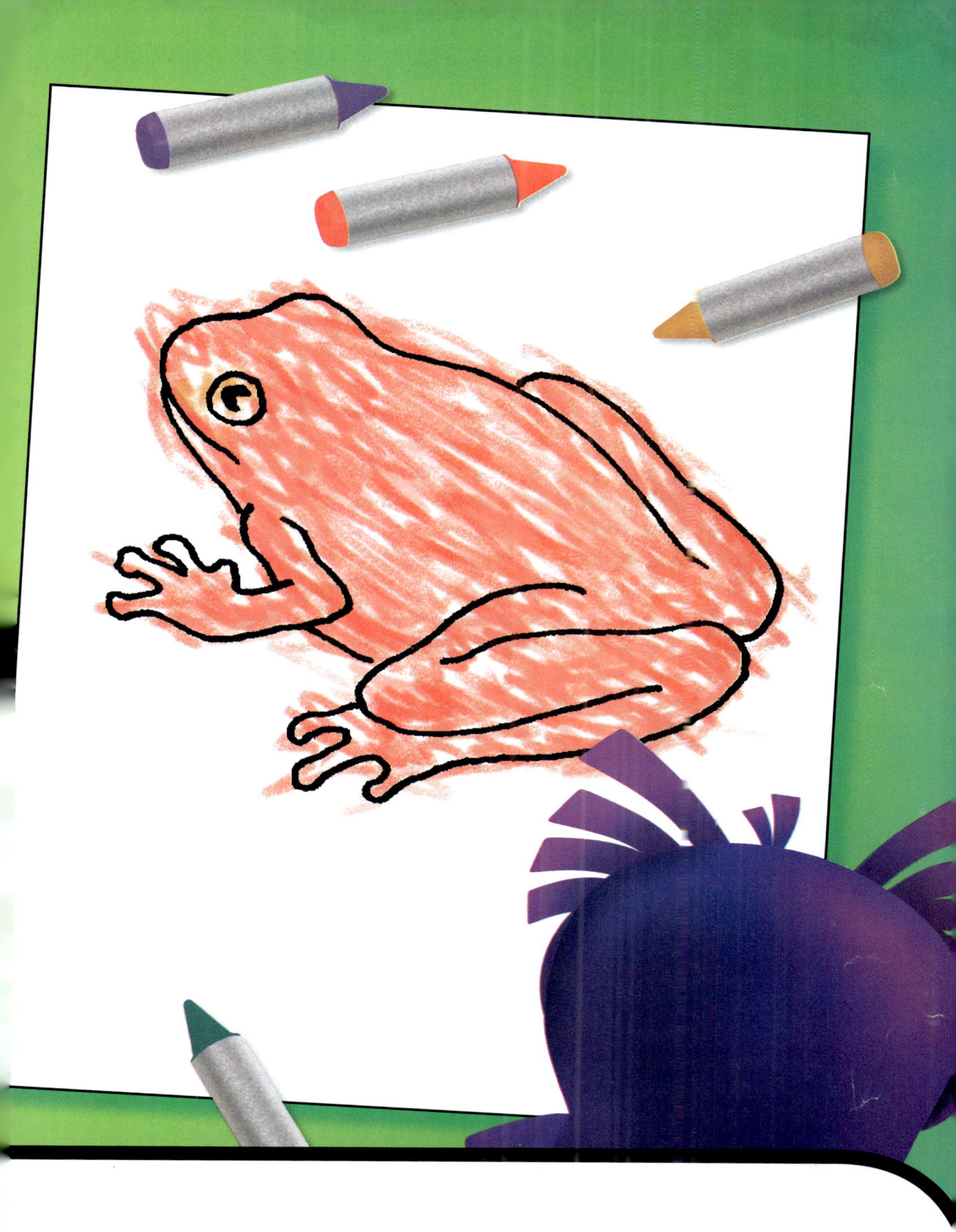

frog

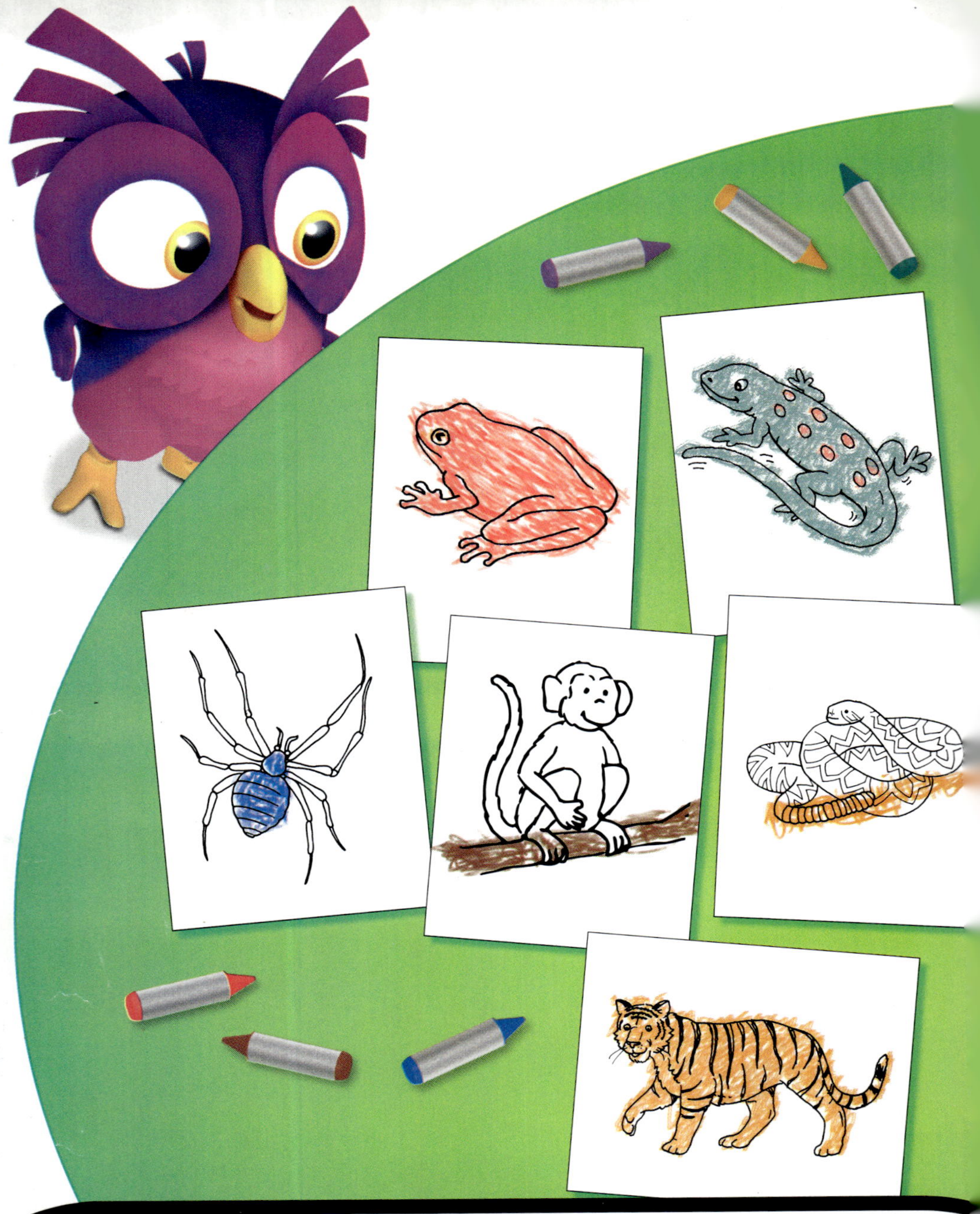

Animals!